Show Me INSECTS

My First Picture Encyclopedia

by Mari Schuh

Consultant:

Laura Jesse, PhD
Plant & Insect Diagnostic Clinic
Iowa State University Extension

CAPSTONE PRESS
a capstone imprint

A+ Books are published by Capstone Press,
1710 Roe Crest Drive, North Mankato, Minnesota 56003.
www.capstonepub.com

Library of Congress Cataloging-in-Publication Data
Schuh, Mari C., 1975–
 Show me insects : my first picture encyclopedia / by Mari Schuh.
  p. cm. — (A+. My first picture encyclopedias.)
 Summary: "Defines through text and photos core terms related to insects"—Provided
  by publisher.
 ISBN 978-1-4296-8569-6 (library binding)
 ISBN 978-1-62065-929-8 (paper over board)
 ISBN 978-1-62065-196-4 (ebook PDF)
 1. Insects–Encyclopedias. I. Title.

 QL462.3.S38 2013
 595.703–dc23   2012003760

Editorial Credits

Kristen Mohn, editor; Tracy Davies McCabe, designer; Svetlana Zhurkin, media researcher; Laura Manthe, production specialist

Photo Credits

Alamy: Arco Images GmbH (spittlebug), 6, blickwinkel, 19 (top), 22 (top), Les Gibbon, 23 (bottom front), Nigel Cattlin, 25 (middle left), Premaphotos, 29 (top middle), Rolf Nussbaumer Photograp[h], 26 (bottom), Scott Camazine, 29 (top right); Brand X Pictures, 4 (top left); CDC: James Gathany, 22 (bottom); Dreamstime: Alexandra Nitsche, 29 (middle), Andrey Prokuronov, 19 (bottom right), Bevanward, 15 (top left), Donviper, 14 (top), Hakoar, 15 (top right), Henrikhl (aphid), 7, Holger Leyrer, 19 (bottom left), Isselee, 27 (middle left), Photomyeye, 21 (top right), Photoncatcher, 11 (midd[le] right), Stef Bennett, 19 (middle right), Vasiliy Vishnevskiy, 31 (bottom left); iStockphotos: alohaspirit, 7 (top right), Dragisa Savic, 14 (right), fotosav, 28 (top), Michael Westhoff, 27 (top left), Olena Chernenko, 18 (top left), Paul Erickson, 31 (top left); Minden Pictures: Satoshi Kuribayashi, 23 (top right); Nature Picture Library: Kim Taylor, 25 (top left), 26 (top right), Premaphotos, 29 (bottom left); Newscom: Danita Delimont Photography/David Northcott, 20 (top left), Danita Delimont Photography/Jaynes Gallery/Dave Welling, 29 (top left); Shutterstock: Alex Staroseltsev (ladybug), cover, 5 (top), alle, 11 (top right), alslutsky, 9 (left), Ammit, 12 (bottom left), Andrii Muzyka, 17 (top left), Anest (hornet), cover, 1, Anita Patterson Peppers, 25 (top right), Anna Subbotina, 5 (bottom left), Anson0618, 5 (middle), Attl Tibor, 24 (top), Beth Van Trees, 13 (bottom middle and right), Bogdan Horia, 12 (middle right), Bruce MacQueen, 15 (bottom), Charles Shapiro, 14 (bottom), Chris Pole, 19 (middle left), Connie Wade, 24 (middle), Cosmin Manci, 5 (top right), 6 (middle left), Dean Evangelista, 29 (bottom right), Dennis Katz, 27 (top right), Dr. Morley Read, 13 (top left), Eduard Kyslynskyy, 21 (middle left), Emily Goodwin, 15 (middle), Eric Isselée, cover (praying mantis and caterpillar), 6 (middle right), 7 (top left), 18 (bottom), 28 (bottom left), Evgeniy Ayupov, 4 (bottom left), Four Oaks, 23 (middle right), Hagit Berkovich, 6 (top left), hellea, 17 (top right), Henrik Larsson, 11 (top left), 21 (top left), 23 (top middle), 30 (top right and bottom), Horatiu Bota (beetle), cover, Hordlena, 12 (bottom right), Jackiso (leaves), 21, Jamie Roach, 13 (top right), Jens Stolt, 12 (top), Jubal Harshaw, 9 (middle right), kesipun, 31 (bottom right), Kirsanov, back cover (right), 8 (right), 17 (bottom right), Kletr (mosquito), cover, back cover, 1, 2, 3, Konstantin Sutyagin (fly), cover, back cover, 1, 2, Kromkrathog (grass), 20, kurt_G, 10 (right), 12 (bottom middle), 16 (top), 28 (middle right), leungchopan, 20 (back), Lukáš Hejtman, 22 (middle), Martin Lehmann, 26 (top left), matzsoca, 31 (top middle), Mau Horn, 16 (bottom), maxstockphoto, 7 (middle left), Melinda Fawver, 6 (bottom right), 7 (bottom left), 25 (bottom), Michael Biehler, 17 (bottom left), Mihail Anatolevich Orlov, 31 (middle left), newphotoservice, 7 (middle right), Nicola Dal Zotto, 7 (bottom right), night_cat, 5 (bottom right), Oleksiy Fedorov, 23 (top left), Olena Istomina, 8 (left), Oranong, 27 (bottom right), p.studio66, 31 (top right), Pan Xunbin, 5 (top left), Peter Waters, 4 (top right), 6 (leafhopper), PetrP (cricket), 6, Photobank, 21 (bottom right), PSno7, 23 (bottom back), pzAxe, 17 (middle), Ron Rowan Photography, 30 (top left), R-studio (torn paper), cover, 1, sellingpix, 18 (top right), Sofiaworld, 11 (bottom), ssguy (insect eggs), cover, 10 (left), Steve Bower, 24 (bottom), Steve Collender, 13 (bottom left), Suzan Oschmann, 31 (middle right), Tom Burlison, cover (butterfly), 27 (middle right), Triff (wasp), cover, back cover, 1, 2, 9, Tyler Fox, 25 (middle right), vblinov, 20 (top right), 27 (bottom left), vnlit, 4 (bottom right), wacpan (grasshopper), 6, Yaroslav, 23 (middle left)

Note to Parents, Teachers, and Librarians

My First Picture Encyclopedias provide an early introduction to reference materials for young children. These accessible, visual encyclopedias support literacy development by building subject-specific vocabularies and research skills. Stimulating format, inviting content, and phonetic aids assist and encourage young readers.

The author dedicates this book to her nephews, Alex and David Schuh of Tracy, Minnesota.

Printed in the United States of America in North Mankato, Minnesota.

092012   006933CGS13

Table of Contents

Get to Know Insects

Insects are a group of small animals in the animal kingdom. There are more than one million kinds of insects—more than any other animal in the world. Scientists have divided the insects into groups. Read on to get the buzz on some of these bug groups!

butterflies and moths

insects with four big wings that have tiny scales on them; when they are young, these insects are caterpillars

ants, bees, and wasps

many of these kinds of insects live and work in groups; some insects in this group have stingers

termites

small insects that eat wood; termites have a soft body and a thick waist

beetles

insects with hard or leathery wings and bodies; there are more kinds of beetles than any other kind of animal in the world; ladybugs and fireflies are types of beetles

cockroaches

(KOK-roh-ches)—black or brown insects with flat, oval bodies and long antennae; cockroaches are good runners and are able to squeeze into small places

flies and mosquitoes

(muh-SKEE-tohs)—two-winged insects that start life in wet places; includes houseflies, fruit flies, and biting midges

dragonflies and damselflies

insects with long, thin bodies, large eyes, and strong jaws; they hunt other insects for food

cicadas (sih-KAY-dahs), spittlebugs, and leafhoppers

insects that eat plant sap and can make noise; leafhoppers and spittlebugs are excellent jumpers

fleas

small insects without wings that drink blood from animals; there are about 2,500 known kinds of fleas in the world

walkingsticks

long, thin, plant-eating insects that look like sticks or twigs; these insects usually move slowly

grasshoppers, crickets, and katydids

large insects with strong, powerful back legs for jumping; there are more than 25,000 known kinds of insects in this group

mantids

large insects with folded front legs, two long antennae, and heads that can turn from side to side; the praying mantis belongs in this group

aphids (AY-fids), scales, mealybugs, and whiteflies

small insects that are often thought of as plant pests; they travel very little and some spend their lives on a single plant; scales, mealybugs, and whiteflies have a waxy coating to protect themselves

What Is Not an Insect?

non-insects

spiders, ticks, scorpions, and mites are not insects; they have eight legs—insects have six; these non-insects also do not have any wings or antennae

spider

scorpion

tick

mite

Body Parts

Insects have lots of parts that help them live in their world. Insects can look very different, but as adults they all have a few things in common—six legs, three body sections, and two antennae.

jaw

a part of the mouth used to grab, bite, chew, cut, and crush; insect jaws move from side to side

antenna

(an-TEH-nuh)—a feeler on an insect's head used to taste, smell, and feel; antennae (an-TEN-ee) means more than one antenna

exoskeleton

(ek-soh-SKE-luh-tuhn) an insect's hard, waterproof, outer shell; insects have no bones

proboscis

(pruh-BAH-sis)—a mouthpart like a straw for drinking plant juice; a butterfly rolls out its long proboscis to drink flower nectar

thorax

(THOR-ax)—the strong middle section of an insect's body

head

the front section of an insect's body; insect brains are about the size of a pinhead

abdomen

(AB-duh-muhn) the end section of an insect's body

spiracle

(SPY-ruh-kul)—insects breathe through tiny holes called spiracles on the sides of the body

wing

most insects have wings; dragonflies flutter their four wings to fly forward, sideways, and even backward

scales

tiny, hard plates that cover some insects' bodies and wings

Growing Up

Insects start life as tiny eggs. As they grow, some insects simply get bigger. Others go through big changes as they become adults.

stinkbug eggs

egg

an insect's first stage of life; some termite queens can lay 30,000 eggs in one day

nymph

(NIMF)—a young insect that is not yet an adult; some spittlebug nymphs change colors as they go through growth stages

larva

(LAR-vuh)—the second stage of life for some insects; a larva is an eating machine as it grows bigger; larvae (LAR-vee) means more than one larva

caterpillar

the larva of a moth or butterfly; caterpillars look like worms with many legs

maggot

(MAG-uht)—the soft larva of a fly; maggots do not have legs

pupa

(PYOO-puh)—the life stage between a larva and an adult when the insect is covered in a casing; many changes happen during the pupa stage, but the insect moves very little; pupae (PYOO-pee) means more than one pupa

chrysalis

(KRIS-uh-lis)—a butterfly in its pupa stage; the hard chrysalis casing often hangs from a leaf or twig

cocoon

(kuh-KOON)—a silk covering that protects some insects during their pupa stage

metamorphosis

(met-uh-MOR-fuh-sis)
the changes in some
insects' form as they grow
from an egg to an adult

mate

to join together to make
young; dragonflies can
mate while they fly

Two Kinds of Metamorphosis

incomplete metamorphosis

the nymph looks similar to
the adult and there is no
pupa stage;
grasshoppers,
dragonflies, and
crickets have
incomplete
metamorphosis

 nymph

adult

egg

life span

most insects live for just a few weeks, but queen termites may live for 50 years

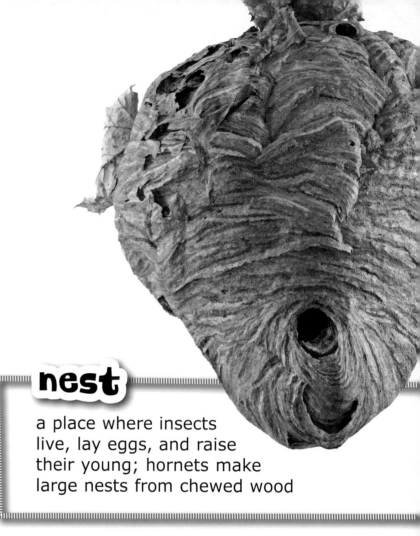

nest

a place where insects live, lay eggs, and raise their young; hornets make large nests from chewed wood

complete metamorphosis

the larva and adult look very different and a pupa is formed; butterflies, ants, and moths have complete metamorphosis

egg

larva

pupa

adult

A Bug's Life

An insect's life may not seem very long to us, but it's just right for a bug. Insects live long enough to molt, migrate, and more!

molt

insects molt or shed exoskeletons many times as they get bigger

migrate

(MYE-grate)—to fly to a place at a certain time of year; each fall, monarch butterflies migrate up to 3,000 miles (4,828 kilometers) to Mexico

hibernate

(HYE-bur-nate)—to sleep all winter; ladybugs gather in large groups to hibernate under tree bark or in buildings

colony

(KAH-luh-nee)—a big group of insects that live and work together; millions of termites can live in one colony

nocturnal

(nok-TUR-nuhl)—active at night; moths often fly around lights at night

social

(SOH-shuhl)—most ants, bees, and termites are social insects; they live and work together, building nests and searching for food

solitary

(SOL-uh-ter-ee)—to live alone; potter wasps live alone in tiny nests that look like vases

Insect Senses

Senses are a big part of an insect's life. Insects sniff out food, watch for enemies, and listen for mates.

compound eye

a big eye that may have thousands of lenses; compound eyes let insects see movement in almost every direction, all at the same time; dragonfly eyes can have as many as 28,000 lenses

ocelli

(oh-SELL-eye) simple eyes that see light and dark; ocelli are found at the top of an insect's head

sensilla

(sen-SILL-uh)—small body parts that help insects sense the world; sensilla that detect smells are usually found in the antennae; other sensilla detect touch or temperature

hearing organ

katydids and crickets hear with hearing organs that are like ears on their front legs; the praying mantis has a hearing organ on its chest

taste receptors

(ri-SEP-turs)—tiny sensors that can detect different tastes; insects can taste salty, bitter, sweet, and sour flavors; butterflies taste with their feet

sensory hair

flies and other insects have tiny hairs on their bodies that can sense movement—they can feel the air move when you reach to swat them!

Johnston's organ

a kind of ear found near the bottom of the antenna on some insects

strands

some male moths have antennae with thin strands that pick up the smell of female moths; some males can smell females several miles away

On the Move

Insects dart across the sky with amazing speed. They scurry along sidewalks and floors. They leap in the air and dive in the water. Insects are almost always on the move!

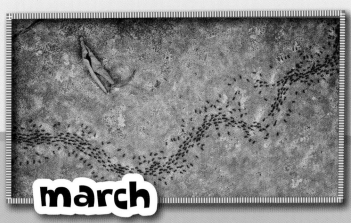

march

to walk together at the same speed; thousands of ants march back to their nest in long lines like highways

swarm

to fly together in big groups; honeybees, grasshoppers, and termites swarm to make new colonies and to mate

rotate

(ROH-tate)—to swing or turn around; a praying mantis can rotate its head to look behind its body for food

row

the water boatman rows across water by using its legs like oars

backswimmer

swim

backswimmers swim upside down

climb

flies climb up and down walls and plants using sticky pads on their feet that act like glue

hover

(HUHV-ur)—to stay in one place in the air; hover flies often hover near flowers like a helicopter

dive

diving beetles dive under water with extra air stored under their wings

skip

to move along lightly; long, thin, hairy legs help water striders skip along the water's surface

Home Sweet Home

Insects are everywhere! Look high and low and you'll likely find an insect habitat—the place in nature where a plant or animal lives.

giant water bug

pond

giant water bugs use a snorkel-like tube to breathe while under water; water scorpions look for food on the bottom of ponds

desert

a dry sandy area with little rain; beetles hide in the desert sand to stay cool during the day

rain forest

a thick forest where a great deal of rain falls; scientists believe 80 percent of the world's insects live in rain forests

bark

many insects make their homes under tree bark; wood-boring beetles can cause serious damage to trees

beehive

a nest where honeybees live with the colony's young; female worker bees keep the beehive clean

burrow

a hole or tunnel in the ground where insects and animals live; mining bees live alone in a little burrow in the ground; small piles of soil mark the burrow's opening

mound

a tall home that termites make from soil, termite waste, and saliva; termite mounds can be taller than a person

What's for Dinner?

Just like people, insects have their favorite foods. But some adult insects, such as luna moths, don't eat anything, because they don't have a mouth!

scavenger

(SKAV-uhn-jer)—an insect that eats dead animals; carrion beetles feast on dead birds and mice

prey

(PRAY)—an animal caught by another animal for food; hungry sand wasps catch prey such as plump caterpillars

mosquito

blood

mosquitoes, biting midges, and some types of flies need blood meals from humans or other animals; the assassin bug may drink up to nine times its weight in blood during a single meal

nectar

a sweet liquid in many flowers; honeybees use nectar to make honey

sap

a liquid in plants and trees that carries water and food

honeydew

sweet liquid waste made by aphids; ants and wasps drink honeydew

pollen

tiny yellow grains in flowers; honeybees gather pollen to eat later at their hive

poop

dung beetles eat animal poop for food!

decaying plants

a dead plant that is breaking down into smaller pieces; young mayflies eat decaying plants

Chatty Critters

Insects can't talk like people do, but they have many ways to get the word out!

chirp

a short, sharp sound; male crickets chirp to call female crickets by rubbing their front wings together

hiss

to make a sound like the letter "s"; Madagascar hissing cockroaches hiss to track down mates and scare away predators

mating call

buzzing, clicking, chirping, or tapping sounds that insects make to find a mate; cicadas have one of the loudest insect mating calls—some can be heard up to 1 mile (1.6 kilometers) away

dance

honeybees dance at their hive to tell other bees where to find pollen or nectar

glow

fireflies give off light to find a mate; each kind of firefly has its own flash pattern

pheromone

(FAIR-uh-mohn)—a chemical an insect gives off; pheromones help insects find mates, alert others to danger, and tell other insects where to go

vibrate

(VYE-brate)—to quickly move back and forth to make a sound; thornbugs talk to each other by shaking their bodies to make tree stems move and vibrate

scent trail

a line of scents that make a path; ants leave scent trails so other ants can find food

Staying Safe

For tiny insects, danger can come from almost anywhere. Read about some of the tricks and traps they use to stay alive.

stinger

a sharp body part on the end of some female insects; bees and wasps have stingers with venom to attack enemies

acid

a strong, sour liquid; wood ants spray enemies with acid from their abdomens

venom

(VEN-uhm)—poison insects make; harvester ants sting with one of the deadliest insect venoms in the world

color patterns

bright colors on some insects warn enemies to stay away; these color patterns tell the enemies that they are not tasty to eat

froth

a bubbly mix of air and liquid that spittlebug nymphs make; the froth keeps the nymphs moist and also keeps away enemies

playing dead

when in danger, ladybugs fall to the ground and pretend to be dead so other animals won't eat them

eyespot

a bright spot on an insect's wing or body that looks like an eye; moths, butterflies, and praying mantises have eyespots that scare enemies because they look like larger animals

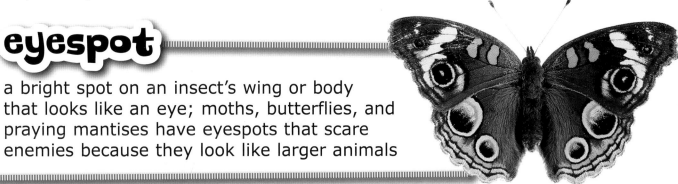

stench

an icky smell; darkling beetles, also known as stinkbugs, stand on their heads and give off a stench when they're bugged

horn

some beetles use horns to fight other beetles

Camouflage and Mimicry

Many insects use camouflage—colors, patterns, and shapes that help them blend in with the background. Others use mimicry, which is to pretend to be another animal in order to stay safe or get food. Can they fool you?

leaves

leaf insects are hard to find in the rain forest because their wings and legs all look like leaves; the wings of some moths and butterflies look like dead leaves

flower

some praying mantises look like flowers; these tricky insects hide in flowers and wait to gobble up prey

buzz

the planthopper buzzes like a stinging wasp when it's caught; it hopes to scare its enemy into letting go

sand

toad bugs have bumpy bodies that blend in with the sand they crawl on

thorn

a sharp growth; thorns help treehoppers look like twigs and branches

twig

stick insects look just like the twigs of a tree

bird droppings

some caterpillars look like bird droppings so other animals won't want to eat them

fake head

some caterpillars have a fake head on their tail; this tricks enemies into attacking the wrong end and protects the caterpillar's real head

snake

the caterpillar of the spicebush swallowtail butterfly scares off enemies by looking like a snake

Helpers and Pests

Insects may be small, but they can be a big help—or a big problem—for people, plants, or other animals.

PESTS

crop
a plant grown for food; beetles and stinkbugs eat soybean crops

Japanese beetles

parasite
(PAIR-uh-site)—an insect that lives in or on another animal and gets food from them; lice are insect parasites that live on human heads or animals and feed on blood

disease
(di-ZEEZ)—some insects spread disease; when mosquitoes bite people, they can sometimes give them a disease called malaria

HELPERS

beeswax

a wax bees make for their hives; people use beeswax to make crayons and candles

food source

many people eat insects for food; people in Africa boil grasshoppers and sprinkle them with salt; in Brazil, people snack on fried queen ants

soil

busy ants help the soil by making tunnels for air and water to move

honey

a sweet food bees make from flower nectar

silk

a soft fiber that silkworms make to form a cocoon; people use silk to make fabric and clothes

protect

to keep safe; wasps protect farmers' crops by eating insect pests that hurt the crops

pollinate

(POL-uh-nate)—to carry pollen between flowers, allowing the flowers to make seeds; without bees, many fruits, vegetables, and flowers would not be pollinated

Read More

Bauer, Jeff. *What Is An Insect?* Science Vocabulary Readers. New York: Scholastic, 2008.

Gibbons, Gail. *Ladybugs.* New York: Holiday House, 2012.

Guillain, Charlotte. *Bugs on the Move.* Comparing Bugs. Chicago: Heinemann Library, 2010.

Salas, Laura Purdie. *Colors of Insects.* Colors All Around. Mankato, Minn.: Capstone Press, 2011.

Titles in this set:

Show me
COMMUNITY HELPERS

Show me
DINOSAURS

Show me
DOGS

Show me
INSECTS

Show me
POLAR ANIMALS

Show me
REPTILES

Show me
SPACE

Show me
TRANSPORTATION

Internet Sites

FactHound offers a safe, fun way to find Internet sites related to this book. All of the sites on FactHound have been researched by our staff.

Here's all you do:

Visit *www.facthound.com*

Type in this code: 9781429685696

Check out projects, games and lots more at
www.capstonekids.com